# Open Court Reading

# Spice Cake

A Division of The McGraw-Hill Companies

Columbus, Ohio

**www.sra4kids.com**

***SRA/McGraw-Hill***

A Division of The **McGraw·Hill** Companies

Copyright © 2002 by SRA/McGraw-Hill.

All rights reserved. Except as permitted under the United States Copyright Act, no part of this publication may be reproduced or distributed in any form or by any means, or stored in a database or retrieval system, without prior written permission from the publisher.

Printed in the United States of America.

Send all inquiries to:
SRA/McGraw-Hill
8787 Orion Place
Columbus, OH 43240-4027

ISBN 0-07-569724-6
3 4 5 6 7 8 9 DBH 05 04 03 02

What is this?
Spice cake?
I can make a nice spice cake, too.

I'll add a shake of this,
and a little pinch of that.

Next I'll add a plate of diced nuts and nine chopped dates.

Then I'll mix in a slice or two of a nice ripe apple.

Stir it a while.
And then bake it...

...and cut a slice for me!